BERNIE SANDERS:
IN HIS OWN WORDS

250 Quotes from America's Political Revolutionary

Edited by Chamois Holschuh

Introduction by Robert Reich

SKYHORSE PUBLISHING

BERNIE SANDERS: IN HIS OWN WORDS

Copyright © 2015 by Skyhorse Publishing, Inc.

Introduction © 2015 by Robert Reich

Illustrations © 2015 by Walker Bragman

Skyhorse Publishing books may be purchased in bulk at special discounts for sales promotion, corporate gifts, fund-raising, or educational purposes. Special editions can also be created to specifications. For details, contact the Special Sales Department, Skyhorse Publishing, 307 West 36th Street, 11th Floor, New York, NY 10018 or info@skyhorsepublishing.com.

Skyhorse® and Skyhorse Publishing® are registered trademarks of Skyhorse Publishing, Inc.®, a Delaware corporation.

Visit our website at www.skyhorsepublishing.com.

10 9 8 7 6 5 4 3 2

Library of Congress Cataloging-in-Publication Data is available on file.

Cover photographs by AFGE and iStock
Cover design by Rain Saukas

Paperback ISBN: 978-1-5107-0714-6
Ebook ISBN: 978-1-5107-0715-3

Printed in the United States of America

TABLE OF CONTENTS

INTRODUCTION

Enthusiasm for Bernie Sanders—and the antiestablishment wave it represents—is not just coming from the "radical left," as some commentators wishing to dismiss it have suggested. In fact, that wave has been growing for years—far longer than the Bernie Sanders campaign itself. Consider that in 1964, just 29 percent of voters believed government was "run by a few big interests looking out for themselves." Now, 79 percent of Americans believe that, according to Gallup.

Meanwhile, for thirty-five years, most Americans haven't seen any gain in their incomes, adjusted for inflation—although the US economy is twice as large as it was thirty-five years ago. Almost all the gains have gone to the richest 1 percent. A disproportionate amount has gone to the richest one-hundredth of one percent. In the "recovery" that began in 2009, all the economic gains went to the top, and the median family lost ground.

It needn't be this way. Globalization and technological advances haven't generated nearly the same savage inequalities in other advanced nations that they have in the United States. That's because our political system has chosen widening inequality. Inequality is less an economic problem than it is a political problem—the consequence of political power concentrating where the money is—giving license to the moneyed interests to siphon off even more of the economy's gains.

We need fundamental reform. And it must restore equal opportunity.

This is not a revolt by the "radical left." It's a revolt by average Americans who are fed up with the direction we're heading.

1

Anyone who is poor in America, or who has borne the scars of discrimination, or who has been marginalized and minimized and bullied, must know we cannot move forward toward a more inclusive society until we confront the savage inequalities of income, wealth, and political power that have taken over our economy and democracy. Reversing them is not sufficient in itself; we must also root out the vestiges of racism and sexism and intolerance. But wresting our economy and democracy back from the moneyed interests is a necessary step.

The media continue to treat Bernie Sanders's campaign as if it's like any other presidential campaign that's organized from the top and reaches downward to find supporters. In reality, his campaign is a movement that started from the grass roots and has reached upward to find Bernie. The challenge for that movement is how to reach outward to millions of others—blacks, Latinos, Independents, even Republicans—and how to turn the enthusiasm into an organization that gets out the vote.

Others confuse Bernie Sanders's surge as a reflection of Democrats' growing unease with Hillary Clinton. I think that's dead wrong. The enthusiasm for Bernie has nothing to do with Hillary. It's about what Bernie is telling America. He's talking about the loss of power of the middle class and poor relative to the powerful and privileged at the top. And he's asking Americans to join together—not just Democrats but Independents and Republicans as well; not just the middle class but also the poor; not just whites but also blacks and Latinos and Asians—in order to wrest power away from the top and reclaim our economy and democracy.

Hillary Clinton would make a fine president, infinitely better than any Republican now running. But Hillary is not a movement. Bernie is.

Some others say they support Bernie, "but he has no chance." I recall people using the same phrase in 2007 and 2008 when they referred to a black man with funny ears and an Arab-sounding name.

2

Introduction

Obviously there is no way of knowing at this juncture whether Bernie Sanders will get the Democratic nomination in 2016 and then win the general election to become president.

But there is no denying the energy and enthusiasm his candidacy has released—a passion for an economy and a democracy responsive to the many, not the few.

Time and again, America has rescued itself. Between 1901 and 1916, during the Progressive Era, we reclaimed our economy and democracy from the robber barons of the Gilded Age. In the New Deal of the 1930s, we retooled our system so it would work for the vast majority. In the 1960s, with the Civil Rights Act, Voting Rights Act, Medicare, Medicaid, and then in 1970 with the Environmental Protection Act, we reformed our democracy further and widened the circle of prosperity.

We will do so again.

> —Robert B. Reich, former Secretary of Labor,
> Chancellor's Professor of Public Policy at the
> University of California at Berkeley, and Senior Fellow
> at the Blum Center for Developing Economies

BERNIE'S CAMPAIGNS: PAST AND PRESENT

"This campaign is not simply about electing me, I hope we accomplish that but that isn't the most important thing. The most important thing is building a political movement in which millions of people who have given up on the political process, including a lot of young people, get involved."

—on his grassroots campaign strategy, July 28, 2015

"People should not underestimate me."

—to the Associated Press on his announcement to run for president, April 30, 2015

"This campaign is not a billionaire-funded campaign. It is a people campaign. We don't take money from billionaires. We don't take money from corporations. Yet we have received more individual contributions than any other campaign. We don't have the money but when people stand together there is nothing we can't accomplish."

—on his presidential campaign, August 11, 2015

"The reason why we are doing well in this campaign is because we are telling the truth."

—on his presidential campaign, August 11, 2015

"This campaign is not about Bernie Sanders. It's about a grassroots movement of Americans standing up and saying: 'Enough is enough. This country and our government belong to all of us, not just a handful of billionaires.'"

—on his presidential campaign, April 30, 2015

"When I was a boy and watched presidents and other candidates on television, it became clear what they were saying didn't make sense to my parents or even me. I came to realize it is right and necessary for people to stand up and oppose what is wrong. I have learned that people will respond if you tell them the truth about how you see the world."

—when asked why he was running for governor of Vermont, October 6, 1976

"We need to be an example to America that a grassroots movement fighting for social justice, fighting for economic democracy, for the rights of all people, rather than just for the very rich is an idea that is as American as apple pie."

—on winning his fourth term as mayor of Burlington, Vermont, 1987

"What I'm trying to do in this campaign is raise issues that very few people talk about and are not going to see on TV or in the newspapers."

—Campaign speech in Keene, New Hampshire, June 6, 2015

"I've never run a negative ad in my life. Why not? First of all, in Vermont, they don't work—and, frankly, I think increasingly around this country they don't work. I really do believe that people want a candidate to come up with solutions to America's problems rather than just attacking his or her opponent. . . . I don't need to spend my life attacking Hillary Clinton or anyone else. I want to talk about my ideas on the issues."

—Interview, "Bernie Sanders Speaks,"
The Nation, July 6, 2015

"Let's be clear. This campaign is not about Bernie Sanders. It is not about Hillary Clinton. It is not about Jeb Bush or anyone else. This campaign is about the needs of the American people, and the ideas and proposals that effectively address those needs."

—Announcement of presidential candidacy,
"Remarks by Sen. Bernie Sanders,"
Burlington Free Press, May 26, 2015

"If ordinary people are to survive in the coming years, it is absolutely imperative that we band together in an organized effort to take control of the institutions which influence how we live."

—on his campaign for mayor of Burlington, Vermont, November 9, 1980

"It is better to show up than to give up."

—on his presidential campaign, June 29, 2015

"We can be a nation where everyone no matter race, their religion, their disability or their sexual orientation realizes the full promise of equality that is our birthright as Americans."

—*Twitter*, August 12, 2015

"If you run a decent and intelligent administration, people are not afraid of the word 'socialism.'"

—after winning his second term as mayor of Burlington, Vermont, March 2, 1983

"This campaign for Congress is about hope. It is saying to the people of Vermont, especially the working people, the elderly people, environmentalists, peace activists, people who year after year feel that they've been knocking their heads against Washington: 'Please don't give up.'"

—announcing bid for Vermont seat in the US House of Representatives, March 20, 1990

"It's not easy changing the world."

—after losing race for Vermont seat in the US House of Representatives, November 9, 1988

"The state of Vermont has a history of sending unconventional representatives, mavericks, to Washington. Over forty years ago, we sent George Aiken there."

> —on announcing his bid for Vermont seat
> in the US House of Representatives,
> March 11, 1988

"They told me: 'Don't you know, Bernie, that Texas is a Republican state?' Well, that's exactly why I'm here."

> —on his presidential campaign visit to
> Texas, July 31, 2015

"Some people told me Louisiana was a conservative state. I guess not."

—on his presidential campaign visit to
Louisiana, July 26, 2015

"Our opponents have the billionaires on their side, but we have the people."

—on his presidential campaign, July 27, 2015

"What we showed tonight was that you can take on the leadership of the Democratic party, the Republican party, the big business community, the local newspaper, and all the big money, and you can beat 'em if you stick together, and we did that."

—on winning his third term as
mayor of Burlington, Vermont, 1985

"It is very easy for a candidate to speak to people who hold the same views. It's harder but important to reach out to others who look at the world differently."

—on being invited to speak at
Liberty University, August 5, 2015

"As for my qualifications, I am not a politician."

—when asked why he was running
for the US Senate, November 24, 1971

ECONOMY, JOBS, AND WEALTH DISTRIBUTION

"[T]he American people are angry . . . Young people who are graduating high school and graduating college, they're going out into the world, they want to become independent, they want to work, and there are no jobs."

—Senate Floor Statement, June 27, 2012

"What the American people are angry about is they understand that they did not cause this recession. Teachers did not cause this recession. Firefighters and police officers who are being attacked daily by governors all over this country did not cause this recession. Construction workers did not cause this recession. This recession was caused by the greed, the recklessness, and illegal behavior of the people on Wall Street."

—Senate Floor Statement, June 27, 2012

"In the United States today we have the most unequal distribution of wealth and income since the 1920s. Now, you're not going to see what I'm talking about on Fox, you're not going to see it on NBC or CBS, but it is important that we discuss this issue because it's one of the most important issues facing America."

—Senate Floor Statement, June 27, 2012

"The system is rigged for the wealthy. The eighty-five richest people in the world own more wealth than the bottom half of the people. I hope this conference will start a serious discussion of about how to change the international financial rules to expand economic opportunity and reduce income inequality and poverty. The global economy has simply failed when so few have so much and so many have so little."

—2015 International Association of Sheet Metal, Air, Rail, and Transportation Workers Conference, July 28, 2015

"In the richest country on the face of the earth, no one who works forty hours a week should be living in poverty."

—Minimum Wage Rally, Washington, DC,
July 22, 2015

"In the year 2015, a job has got to lift workers out of poverty, not keep them in it. The $7.25 an hour federal minimum wage is a starvation wage. It has got to be increased to a living wage!"

—Minimum Wage Rally, Washington, DC,
July 22, 2015

"When workers don't have to worry about how they are going to feed their families or pay the rent, they become better workers. And when low-wage workers get a raise they spend their money in local businesses and that creates more jobs, not less!"

—Minimum Wage Rally, Washington, DC,
July 22, 2015

"A nation is judged by how it cares for its most vulnerable ... American seniors should have the supports available to them to remain in their homes and communities. They deserve to live with dignity and with a sense of security, and the Older Americans Act helps to provide that."

—on the reauthorization of the
Older Americans Act, July 16, 2015

"A nation is judged by how it cares for its most vulnerable including the elderly and children. It is not acceptable that millions of elderly in this country are living in poverty and struggling to feed themselves. Instead of giving tax breaks to billionaires we should be expanding nutrition programs and other services for seniors."

—on results of the Government Accountability Office's study on low-income seniors, June 15, 2015

"If an institution is too big to fail, it is too big to exist."

—on the reinstatement of the Glass-Steagall Act, July 17, 2015

"Too many Americans are working longer and harder without anything to show for their efforts in their paychecks . . . These long hours are straining middle-class workers and their families. Since the 1970s, average salaries for middle-class individuals have dropped even while salaried workers have increased the hours they spend on the job. Strengthening overtime protections will help millions of middle-class families."

—in his letter with Senator Patty Murray, Fair Overtime Pay Letter to the White House, January 31, 2015

"Hard-working retirees should not ever have to doubt their retirement security. We made a commitment forty years ago to workers in this country that companies will never renege on a pension promise. We need to restore that commitment."

—on his bill to amend the Employee Retirement Income Security Act of 1974 and the Internal Revenue Code of 1986, June 18, 2015

"When it comes to basic workplace protections and family benefits, workers in every other major industrialized country in the world get a better deal than workers in the United States. That is wrong . . . Last place is no place for America. It is time to join the rest of the industrialized world by showing the people of this country that we are not just a nation that talks about family values but that we are a nation that is prepared to live up to these ideals."

—on the introduction of the Guaranteed Paid Vacation Act, June 11, 2015

"I have a hard time understanding what world Governor Bush and his billionaire backers live in . . . At a time when more than half of the American people have less than $10,000 in savings, it would be a disaster to cut Social Security benefits by raising the retirement age. It is unacceptable to ask construction workers, truck drivers, nurses and other working-class Americans to work until they are sixty-eight to seventy years old before qualifying for full Social Security benefits."

—on former Florida Governor Jeb Bush's proposal to raise retirement age to 68 or 70, June 3, 2015

"At a time when almost every major corporation in this country has shut down plants and outsourced millions of American jobs, we should not be providing corporate welfare to multi-national corporations through the Export-Import Bank.

"Instead of providing low-interest loans to multi-national companies that are shipping jobs to China and other low-wage countries, we should be investing in small businesses and worker-owned enterprises that want to create jobs in the United States of America. If the Export-Import Bank cannot be reformed to become a vehicle for real job creation in the United States, it should be eliminated."

—on the US Senate's vote on a five-year reauthorization of the Export-Import Bank, June 10, 2015

"The president at Nike headquarters told us that every trade union in America is wrong, that progressives working for years for working families are wrong and that corporate America, the pharmaceutical industry and Wall Street are right. I respectfully disagree.

"This trade agreement would continue the process by which we have been shipping good-paying American jobs to low-wage countries overseas and continue the race to the bottom for American workers."

—on President Obama's visit to Nike's corporate headquarters in relation to the Trans-Pacific Partnership trade deal, May 8, 2015

"[W]e need to protect ourselves from being at the mercy of giant companies that are 'too big to fail,' that is, companies who are so large that their failure would cause systemic harm to the economy. We need to assess which companies fall into this category and insist they are broken up. Otherwise, the American taxpayer will continue to be on the financial hook for the risky behavior, the mismanagement and even the illegal conduct of these companies' executives."

—in his article "Rescue Wall Street—and the Rest of Us," *The Nation*, September 22, 2008

"In America we now have more income and wealth inequality than any other major country on earth, and the gap between the very rich and everyone is wider than at any time since the 1920s. The issue of wealth and income inequality is the great moral issue of our time, it is the great economic issue of our time and it is the great political issue of our time. And we will address it."

—Announcement of presidential candidacy,
"Remarks by Sen. Bernie Sanders,"
Burlington Free Press, May 26, 2015

"This grotesque level of inequality is immoral. It is bad economics. It is unsustainable. This type of rigged economy is not what America is supposed to be about. This has got to change and ... together we will change it.

—Announcement of presidential candidacy,
"Remarks by Sen. Bernie Sanders,"
Burlington Free Press, May 26, 2015

"[A] message to the billionaire class . . . : you can't have it all. You can't get huge tax breaks while children in this country go hungry. You can't continue sending our jobs to China while millions are looking for work. You can't hide your profits in the Cayman Islands and other tax havens, while there are massive unmet needs on every corner of this nation. Your greed has got to end. You cannot take advantage of all the benefits of America, if you refuse to accept your responsibilities."

—Announcement of presidential candidacy,
"Remarks by Sen. Bernie Sanders,"
Burlington Free Press, May 26, 2015

"I think many people have the mistaken impression that Congress regulates Wall Street. In truth, it is the other way around."

—*Twitter*, August 7, 2015

"When a mother must send her sick child to school because she can't afford to stay home, that is not a family value."

—critiquing Republican domination of the term "family values" in conjunction with their political agendas, "The Middle Class: It's Time to Support Real Family Values," www.berniesanders.com, June 17, 2015

"American workers are being denied a benefit that workers in every other advanced economy already enjoy. Europe, Australia, Canada, Japan, New Zealand. . . . we are the only nation that doesn't require employers to provide at least ten percent days of paid vacation time.

"There is no reason for that. Our country is every bit as prosperous as theirs—and it is prosperous because the men and women of this country work so hard."

—on his proposal to require ten days of paid vacation,
"The Middle Class: It's Time to Support Real Family Values,"
www.berniesanders.com, June 17, 2015

"Some people say my economic ideas are radical. You should hear what the pope is saying."

—on the pope's visit to the US, July 28, 2015

"We must convince young people that if they vote in large numbers, we can lower the unemployment they experience with a major jobs program."

—*Twitter*, July 25, 2015

"Warren Buffett has pointed out the unfairness of the fact that he, a multibillionaire, pays a lower effective tax rate than his secretary."

—*Twitter*, July 21, 2015

"We are a nation proud of its dedication to family values. Why can't we ensure that new parents have time to bond with their children?"

—on the limited family benefits of the US workforce, July 18, 2015

"The decision to require companies to disclose how much more CEOs are paid than workers is an important step in the fight against income inequality. The average chief executive in America now makes nearly 300 times more than the average worker—and the gap between the people at the top and working families is growing wider and wider. I hope that shining a spotlight on the disparity will help working families."

—on CEO Pay Rule, August 5, 2015

"We live at a time when most Americans don't have $10,000 in savings, and millions of working adults have no idea how they will ever retire in dignity. God forbid, they are confronted with an unforeseen car accident, a medical emergency, or the loss of a job. It would literally send their lives into an economic tailspin."

—Remarks at the Southern Christian
Leadership Conference, July 25, 2015

"The American people, in general, want change—they want a better deal. A fairer deal. A new deal. They want an America with laws and policies that truly reward hard work with economic mobility."

—Remarks at the Southern Christian
Leadership Conference, July 25, 2015

"[C]ivil rights are not just about voting rights, but economic and social equality—and most importantly, jobs. Fifty years later, it remains the great unfinished business of the civil rights movement."

—Remarks at the Southern Christian
Leadership Conference, July 25, 2015

"The benchmark of full-time work in America should be simple and concrete—that no full-time worker should live in poverty."

—*Twitter*, August 2, 2015

"Despite huge increases in productivity, Americans continue to work some of the longest hours of any country on earth."

—Interview with MSNBC's *The ED Show*, July 9, 2015

"[T]he American consumer does not want the tomatoes they eat to be picked by workers who are grossly mistreated and underpaid."

—while visiting farmers in Immokalee, Florida, 2008

"If the minimum wage had kept pace with productivity, it would be more than $16 per hour today."

—June 16, 2015

"How does it happen that despite huge gains in technology and productivity the average American today is working longer hours for lower wages? How does it happen that median family income today is almost $5,000 less than in 1999, while 99 percent of all new income is going to the top 1 percent?"

—May 4, 2015

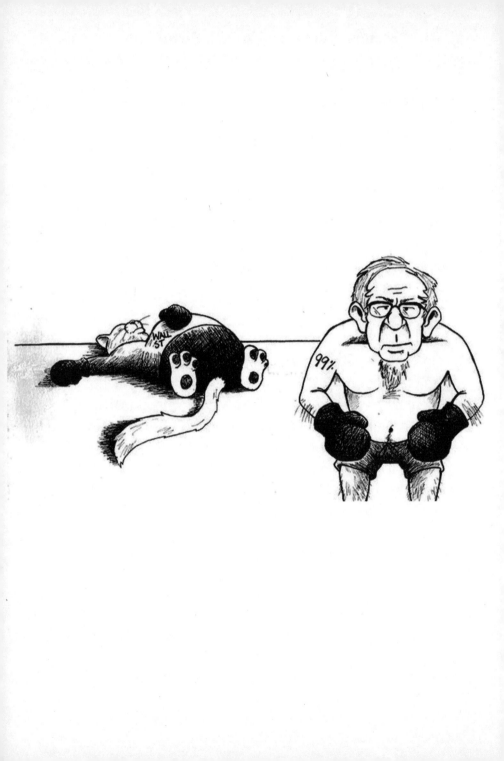

POLITICS, CAMPAIGNS, AND VOTING

"I think the discontent of the American people is far, far greater than the pundits understand."

—Interview, "Bernie Sanders Speaks," *The Nation*, July 6, 2015

"We must remember that the struggle for our rights is not a struggle for one day, or one year, or one generation—it is the struggle of a lifetime, and one that must be fought by every generation."

—Remarks at the Southern Christian Leadership Conference, July 25, 2015

"Either elected officials respond to the needs and views of an involved electorate, or they don't remain elected."

—June 8, 2015

"Democracy is one person, one vote and a full discussion of the issues that affect us. Oligarchy is billionaires buying elections, voter suppression and a concentrated corporate media determining what we see, hear, and read."

—May 27, 2015

"Today virtually no piece of legislation can get passed unless it has the OK from corporate America."

—May 22, 2015

"Most Americans grew up believing that in America the majority rules. They also believe that this country deserves a Senate that is not dysfunctional and unable to address the needs of the American people. Unfortunately, in recent years the Republican minority has engaged in an unprecedented level of obstructionism. They have used the filibuster hundreds of times to delay or block the president's nominees and to stop legislation from even being considered. Today's decision by the Senate to let the majority rule on votes to confirm judges, cabinet secretaries, and other senior administration officials is a step in the right direction toward ending dysfunction in the Senate."

—Statement on Majority Rule in the Senate,
November 21, 2013

"Politics in a democratic society should not be treated like a baseball game, a game show or a soap opera. The times are too serious for that."

—Announcement of presidential candidacy,
"Remarks by Sen. Bernie Sanders,"
Burlington Free Press, May 26, 2015

"In 1936, when Roosevelt ran for reelection, he welcomed the hatred of what he called 'the economic royalists'—today, they're the billionaire class—and I'm prepared to do that as well. That's the kind of language the American people are ready to hear."

—Interview, "Bernie Sanders Speaks,"
The Nation, July 6, 2015

"It is extremely undemocratic that forty-one percent of
the US Senate can thwart the will of the American people,
the president, the House of Representatives and a strong
majority of the Senate. While individual senators will always
have great clout, no one senator should be able to bring the
US government to a halt at one of the most perilous periods
in American history."

—on the need for Senate reform,
in his article "Blueprint for Dems,"
The Nation, January 14, 2010

"Now, I may not be the greatest political strategist in the world, but I don't know how you win elections by ignoring the ideas of the progressives who have worked hardest at the grassroots level for your victories, or the trade unions that have provided significant financial support and door-to-door volunteers for Democratic campaigns. I don't know how you succeed politically when you insult women, who far more than men consistently provide you with great margins of support. How do you preserve a big majority in Congress when you fail to be aggressive in protecting the interests of seniors, a huge voting bloc in off-presidential-year elections? In other words, it should not surprise anyone that the Democrats are in serious trouble."

—on Democrats' attempt to be bipartisan
during Obama's presidency, in his article
"Blueprint for Dems," *The Nation*, January 14, 2010

"When one family spends more money than both parties, that is not democracy, that is oligarchy."

—on the Koch brothers, August 9, 2015

"We can learn from the past. The last time our nation faced economic challenges as great as our own, Franklin Roosevelt embraced progressive social policies and major financial and economic reform. The nation did not ignore or forget his commitment to help American families, provide aid to the disadvantaged and take on the moneyed powers of Wall Street. Roosevelt's greatest political legacy was to build a coalition of Americans from across the country who understood that, if they stood together under a progressive banner, life could be better for the average person. Now is the time to remember that lesson."

—in his article "Blueprint for Dems,"
The Nation, January 14, 2010

"If you ask me about my views on the environment, on women's rights, on gay rights, I am liberal. I don't have a problem with that at all. Some of my best friends are liberal."

—interview, CNN's *Newsroom*, 2009

"Today's Supreme Court decision is an important step in the fight against voter suppression. When congressional districts are controlled by partisanship it is bad for voters and our democracy. Allowing non-partisan commissions to draw district lines will help combat the hyper-partisan gerrymandering we have seen in some states. We still must go further—it's time to restore the Voting Rights Act, expand early voting periods and make it easier for people to vote, not harder."

—on the Supreme Court decision in
*Arizona State Legislature v. Arizona Independent
Redistricting Commission*, June 29, 2015

"Election Day should be a national holiday so that everyone has the time and opportunity to vote. While this would not be a cure-all, it would indicate a national commitment to create a vibrant democracy."

—on the 50th anniversary of the
Voting Rights Act, August 6, 2015

"In America, everybody who is eligible to vote is entitled to vote. That is American democracy."

—on the 50th anniversary of the
Voting Rights Act, August 6, 2015

"If we believe in a vibrant democracy, we want to have the highest voter turnout in the world."

—on the 50th anniversary of the Voting Rights Act, August 6, 2015

"The Supreme Court's 2013 decision gutting the Voting Rights Act was a shameful step backward. The critical civil rights law which protected voters in places with a history of discrimination is as necessary today as it was in the era of Jim Crow laws. We should do everything possible to guarantee the right to vote, not make it harder for people to cast ballots. That's why I strongly support the Voting Rights Advancement Act of 2015."

—on restoring the Voting Rights Act, June 24, 2015

"Voter ID laws aren't intended to discourage fraud, they are intended to discourage voting. They have worked."

—*Twitter*, July 25, 2015

"[T]he American people are becoming increasingly alienated from the political process; 63 percent of the American people didn't vote last November. I'm looking for ways to bring them into a serious discussion about serious issues. When we do that, the Republican agenda will be exposed for the disaster it is."

—on wanting to debate with Republican presidential candidates, interview, "Bernie Sanders Speaks," *The Nation*, July 6, 2015

"These are the last days of the Bush administration, the most dishonest and incompetent in modern American history. It is imperative that, at this important moment, Congress stand up for the middle class and for fiscal integrity. The future of our country is at stake."

—in his article "Rescue Wall Street—and the Rest of Us," *The Nation*, September 22, 2008

"The current campaign system is corrupt and amounts to legalized bribery."

—*Twitter*, August 4, 2015

"In my view, a corporation is not a person. . . . Corporations should not be able to go into their treasuries and spend millions and millions of dollars on a campaign in order to buy elections."

—"Saving Our Democracy,"
The Huffington Post, December 8, 2011

"If elected president, I will have a litmus test in terms of my nominee to be a Supreme Court justice. And that nominee will say that we are all going to overturn this disastrous Supreme Court decision on Citizens United because that decision is undermining American democracy."

—Interview, CBS's *Face the Nation*, May 10, 2015

"Free speech does not equal the ability of people to buy elections."

—*Twitter*, July 31, 2015

"Politics is about people coming together to improve the lives of all Americans, not just wealthy contributors."

—*Twitter*, July 30, 2015

"When congressional districts are controlled by partisanship it is bad for voters and our democracy."

—*Twitter,* June 29, 2015

"In Vermont and at our town meetings we know what American democracy is supposed to be about. It is one person, one vote—with every citizen having an equal say—and no voter suppression. And that's the kind of American political system we have to fight for and will fight for in this campaign."

—Announcement of presidential candidacy,
"Remarks by Sen. Bernie Sanders,"
Burlington Free Press, May 26, 2015

"The right to vote is preservative of all other rights."

—Remarks at the Southern Christian
Leadership Conference, July 25, 2015

"The Supreme Court's 2013 decision gutting the Voting
Rights Act was a shameful step backward."

—*Twitter*, August 9, 2015

"The very rich get richer, everyone else poorer. And Republicans who take campaign money from billionaires have nothing significant to say."

—on the Republican presidential primary debates,
Twitter, August 6, 2015

"In my view, we should learn from history. We should understand that when democracy fails and people cannot get what they voted for because of outside forces it leads to contempt for democracy and people vote for parties like Golden Dawn."

—on the Greek financial crisis,
2015 International Association of Sheet Metal,
Air, Rail, and Transportation Workers
Conference, July 28, 2015

"Listen to R[epublican]s talk about military funding and remember what Eisenhower said about power of the military-industrial complex."

—on the Republican presidential primary debates,
Twitter, August 6, 2015

"Still waiting. Will Fox ask if it's appropriate for billionaires to buy elections?"

—on the Republican presidential primary debates,
Twitter, August 6, 2015

"You know how far right the GOP has gone when its so-called 'moderate' candidate Jeb Bush is talking about 'phasing out' Medicare."

—*Twitter*, July 24, 2015

"The ruling has radically changed the nature of our democracy. It has further tilted the balance of power toward the rich and the powerful . . . History will record that the Citizens United decision is one of the worst in the history of our country."

—"Saving Our Democracy,"
The Huffington Post, December 8, 2011

"I will be introducing legislation which calls for public funding of elections, which will enable any candidate, regardless of his or her political views, to run for office without being beholden to powerful special interests."

—August 4, 2015

". . . Not one word about economic inequality, climate change, Citizens United or student debt. That's why the Republicans are so out of touch."

—on the Republican presidential debate, *Twitter*, August 6, 2015

"All across this country people are sick and tired of establishment politics, establishment economics and they want real change. The people of America understand that corporate greed is destroying our country, and that much of the mainstream media is prepared to talk about everything except for what is the most important."

—campaign rally at the University of Washington, August 8, 2015

"The defining principle of American democracy is one person, one vote—with every citizen having an equal say—and no voter suppression. And that's the kind of American political system we have to fight for."

—Remarks at the Southern Christian Leadership Conference, July 25, 2015

"The US is one of the few countries which puts the onus of registration on the voter, not the state. This is ridiculous."

—Remarks at the Southern Christian
Leadership Conference, July 25, 2015

"I do not believe that billionaires should be able to buy politicians."

—Interview, CBS's *Face the Nation*, May 10, 2015

"Freedom of speech does not mean the freedom to buy the United States government."

—*Twitter*, August 12, 2015

"There is a lot of sentiment that enough is enough, that we need fundamental changes, that the establishment—whether it is the economic establishment, the political establishment, or the media establishment—is failing the American people."

—"An Economic Agenda for America:
A Conversation with Bernie Sanders,"
Center for Effective Public Management at Brookings,
Feburary 9, 2015

"It is time to end the politics of division in this country of politicians playing one group of people against another."

—*Twitter*, August 12, 2015

"I think we proved something to the country. People with strong differences don't have to kill each other or defame each other, but they can disagree and do their job as best that they can."

—in his farewell address upon leaving
the mayoral office of
Burlington, Vermont, April 4, 1989

EQUALITY

Class

"The billionaires of America are on the warpath. They want more and more and more."

—Full Congressional Record Transcript of Sanders Filibuster: The Economy, December 10, 2010

"Our nation cannot survive morally or economically when so few have so much while so many have so little."

—on his proposal to increase the estate tax, June 25, 2015

"As Franklin Delano Roosevelt reminded us, a nation's greatness is judged not by what it provides to the most well-off, but how it treats the people most in need. And that's the kind of nation we must become."

> —Announcement of presidential candidacy,
> "Remarks by Sen. Bernie Sanders,"
> *Burlington Free Press,* May 26, 2015

"We need to educate, organize and mobilize the working families of our country to stand up for their rights."

> —*Twitter,* July 29, 2015

"[T]he United States must not become an oligarchy in which a handful of wealthy and powerful families control the destiny of our nation. Too many people, from the inception of this country, have struggled and died to maintain our democratic vision. We owe it to them and to our children to maintain it."

—in his article "No to Oligarchy,"
The Nation, July 22, 2010

"While the middle class disappears and poverty increases the wealthiest people in our country are not only doing extremely well, they are using their wealth and political power to protect and expand their very privileged status at the expense of everyone else."

—in his article "No to Oligarchy,"
The Nation, July 22, 2010

74

Equality

"The reality is that the middle class in America today is collapsing and poverty is increasing."

> — "Bernie Sanders Tells Obama, 'We Will Not Balance
> the Budget on the Backs of Working Families,'"
> *The Nation*, June 27, 2011

"We cannot continue to ignore the crisis of youth unemployment in America. We are talking about the future of an entire generation. . . . We have got to make sure that young people in Washington, DC, and all over this country have the opportunity to earn a paycheck and to make it into the middle class."

> —Statement on Employ Young
> Americans Act, June 4, 2015

"Why is it that millions of Americans are working longer hours for lower wages while a handful of billionaires do unbelievably well?"

—May 12, 2015

"The average American today is underpaid, overworked and stressed out as to what the future will bring for his or her children. For many, the American dream has become a nightmare."

—in his article "No to Oligarchy," *The Nation*, July 22, 2010

"Poverty in America is in fact very expensive . . . If people don't have access to health care, if they don't have access to education, if they don't have access to jobs and affordable housing then we end up paying not only in terms of human suffering and the shortening of life expectancy but in actual dollars."

—November 20, 2013

"We know that the most effective solutions for homelessness combine safe and affordable housing with essential services to help people get back on their feet."

—Joint statement with Senator Patrick Leahy and Representative Peter Welch on federal funds for community development in Vermont, March 30, 2015

"When you look at the basic necessities of life—education, health care, nutrition—there must be a guarantee that people receive what they need in order to live a dignified life."

—*Twitter*, August 5, 2015

"And I think what the American people are saying is enough is enough. This country, this great country, belongs to all of us. It cannot continue to be controlled by a handful of billionaires who apparently want it all. You know, I, for the love of me, I cannot understand why people who have billions of dollars are compulsively driven for more and how many people have got to die because they don't go to a doctor because you want to avoid paying your taxes?"

—Senate Floor Statement, June 27, 2012

"Well, that's not what America is about. That's not what people fought and died to create. With that, we have got a fight on our hands. The job of the United States national is to represent the middle-class families of this country, all of the people, and not just the super-rich. I hope we can begin to do that."

—Senate Floor Statement, June 27, 2012

Race

"America becomes a greater nation, a stronger nation, when we stand together as one people and in a very loud and clear voice, we say 'no' to all forms of racism and bigotry."

—at national conference of the
National Council of La Raza, July 13, 2015

"We must pursue policies that transform this country into a nation that affirms the value of its people of color. That starts with addressing the four central types of violence waged against black and brown Americans: physical, political, legal and economic."

—on racial justice, www.berniesanders.com

"We want a nation where young black men and women can live without fear of being falsely arrested, beaten or killed. #BlackLivesMatter"

—*Twitter*, July 19, 2015

"If current trends continue, one in three black males born today can expect to spend time in prison during his lifetime. This is an unspeakable tragedy."

—Statement on Employ Young Americans Act, June 4, 2015

"I do not separate the civil-rights issue from the fact that 50 percent of African-American young people are either unemployed or underemployed. Remember the March on Washington—what was it about? 'Jobs and Freedom.' The issue that Dr. King raised all the time was: This is great if we want to desegregate restaurants or hotels, but what does it matter if people can't afford to go to them? That's still the issue today."

—Interview, "Bernie Sanders Speaks,"
The Nation, July 6, 2015

"Those are twin issues. Combating institutional racism but dealing with economic justice issues so that our kids have jobs rather than ending up in jail. That's a message I'm bringing all over the country."

—on the need to address unemployment among young African Americans, "Sanders More Vocal on Racial Justice Issues," *Burlington Free Press*, July 30, 2015

"One of the great crises facing this country, a crisis that we talk too little about, is youth unemployment in general and black and Hispanic youth unemployment in particular. Today, in our country, youth unemployment is 17 percent and black youth unemployment (ages 16–19) is 27 percent. This is unacceptable, this is having a huge impact on our society, and this cannot be allowed to continue."

—Statement on Employ Young Americans Act,
June 4, 2015

"On criminal justice reform and the need to fight racism there is no other candidate who will fight harder."

—*Twitter*, August 8, 2015

"The answer to unemployment and poverty is not and cannot be the mass incarceration of young African Americans. It's time to bring hope and economic opportunity to communities across the country."

—Statement on Employ Young Americans Act,
June 4, 2015

"The Charleston church killings are a tragic reminder of the ugly stain of racism that still taints our nation. This senseless violence fills me with outrage, disgust and a deep, deep sadness. The hateful killing of nine people praying inside a church is a horrific reminder that, while we have made significant progress in advancing civil rights in this country, we are far from eradicating racism. Our thoughts and prayers are with the families and their congregation."

—on the Charleston church shootings, June 18, 2015

"Of course the majority of people of color are trying to work hard, play by the rules and raise their children. But there are neighborhoods where mothers are afraid to let their children outside for fear of gang violence and drugs. And they are also afraid of their children being targeted by the police because of the color of their skin. No person should have to worry that a routine interaction with law enforcement will end in violence or death."

—Remarks at the Southern Christian Leadership Conference, July 25, 2015

LGBTQ

"You can't claim to support equality and not support equal rights."

—on Supreme Court's consideration
of gay marriage, April 27, 2015

"Probably the most alarming aspect of the Nixon administration has been the gradual erosion of freedoms and the sense of what freedom really means. The Liberty Union believe that there are entirely too many laws that regulate human behavior. Let us abolish all laws which attempt to impose a particular brand of morality or 'right' on people. Let's abolish all laws dealing with abortion, drugs, sexual behavior (adultery, homosexuality, etc.)."

—written while campaigning for US Senate,
"A Letter from Bernie Sanders," *The Freeman*, 1972

"Of course all citizens deserve equal rights. It's time for the Supreme Court to catch up to the American people and legalize gay marriage."

> —on Supreme Court's consideration
> of gay marriage, April 28, 2015

"This decision is a victory for same-sex couples across our country as well as all those seeking to live in a nation where every citizen is afforded equal rights."

> —on Supreme Court ruling in favor of same-sex marriage,
> *Twitter*, June 26, 2015

"Today the Supreme Court fulfilled the words engraved upon its building: 'Equal justice under law.'"

—on Supreme Court ruling in favor of same-sex marriage, *Twitter*, June 26, 2015

"For far too long our justice system has marginalized the gay community and I am very glad the Court has finally caught up to the American people."

—on Supreme Court ruling in favor of same-sex marriage, June 26, 2015

"People have a right to love each other, regardless of one's sexual orientation. I voted against the DOMA act, the so-called Defense of Marriage Act, way back in 1996 that was signed by President Clinton, because I think, if people are in love, they should be able to get married in this country in fifty states in America."

—Interview, CNN, July 5, 2015

"I am proud to represent the first state in the country to allow civil unions and the first state where the Legislature allowed same-sex marriage without a court order."

—May 9, 2012

"We've got to end LGBT discrimination in the workplace. Vermont did this twenty-two years ago when it passed one of the first state laws in the country protecting lesbian and gay workers. Congress should have acted long ago, but Republicans have blocked action."

—July 18, 2014

Women

"When you tell a woman that she cannot control her own body, that's extremism."

—*Twitter*, August 4, 2015

"The attempt by Republicans to cut off support for Planned Parenthood is an attack on women's health."

—*Twitter*, July 31, 2015

"Simply stated it is an outrage that millions of women in this country give birth and then are forced back to work because they don't have the income to stay home with their newborn babies."

—on the Guaranteed Paid Vacation Act, June 11, 2015

"The campaign by Senate Republicans to defund Planned Parenthood is a waste of valuable time in the Senate. Instead of trying to take away health care from millions of women, we should be passing legislation to provide family and medical leave to all of our families. We should also pass pay equity legislation so that women do not continue to earn seventy-eight cents on the dollar compared to men."

—after voting against a motion to debate a decrease in funding for Planned Parenthood, August 3, 2015

"Will Fox and the R[epublican]s talk about pay equity for women workers who make 78 cents on the dollar compared to men? Waiting."

—on the Republican presidential primary debates, *Twitter*, August 6, 2015

"A living wage should not only be fair, it should be equitable. That is why we must establish pay equity for women workers by law."

—*Twitter*, August 8, 2015

"Brothers, we need to stand with our sisters and fight for pay equity."

—*Twitter*, August 10, 2015

ENVIRONMENT

"Protecting our environment is not a radical idea. It is a moral responsibility."

—May 23, 2015

"The fossil fuel industry is destroying the planet with impunity and getting rich while doing it."

—*Twitter*, July 31, 2015

"Climate change threatens the planet, and we have a major political party denying its reality."

—*Twitter*, July 23, 2015

"Why is it that Republicans are willing to bail out Wall Street but refuse to act on climate change? Let's be honest. If the environment were a bank it would have been saved by now."

—June 9, 2015

"Unless we take bold action to reverse climate change, our children, grandchildren and great-grandchildren are going to look back on this period in history and ask a very simple question: Where were they? Why didn't the United States of America, the most powerful nation on earth, lead the international community in cutting greenhouse gas emissions and preventing the devastating damage that the scientific community was sure would come?"

—Bernie Sanders, *Facebook*, April 23, 2013

"The scientific community tells us very clearly if we're going to reverse climate change and the great dangers it poses for the planet we must move aggressively to transform our energy system away from fossil fuels to sustainable energy."

—in his Introduction of Low Income Solar Act of 2015, July 7, 2015

"At a time when our planet is warming due to climate change, the last thing our environment needs is more drilling. What we need is for Congress and the White House to move toward clean energy such as solar, wind and biomass."

—on oil drilling in the Arctic Ocean, May 28, 2015

"While the cost of solar panels has gone down in recent years, it is still out of reach for millions of low-income families that need it the most. Families across this country struggle to pay electricity bills and access to solar energy can help reduce these costs."

—in his Introduction of Low Income Solar Act of 2015, July 7, 2015

"Pope Francis's powerful message on climate change should change the debate around the world and become a catalyst for the bold actions needed to reverse global warming. The pope helps us all see how those with the least among us will fare the worst from the consequences of climate change. I very much appreciate that the Republican leadership has invited the pope to address Congress. I hope they listen to what he has to say. Denying the science related to climate change is no longer acceptable."

—on Pope Francis's encyclical on climate change, June 18, 2015

"There is a moral responsibility that we must accept to transform our energy system. It cannot be ignored."

—Interview, "Bernie Sanders Speaks,"
The Nation, July 6, 2015

"In fact, the truth rarely uttered in Washington is that with strong governmental leadership the crisis of global warming is not only solvable; it can be done while improving the standard of living of the people of this country and others around the world. And it can be done with the knowledge and technology that we have today; future advances will only make the task easier."

—in his article "Global Warming is Reversible,"
The Nation, December 10, 2007

"As the nation at last confronts global warming, it is no time for denial, greed, cynicism or pessimism. It is a time for vision and international leadership. It is a time for transforming our energy system from the polluting and carbon-emitting technologies of the nineteenth century into the unlimited and extraordinary energy possibilities of the twenty-first. When we do that we will not only solve the global warming crisis; we will open up unimaginable opportunities for improving life all over the planet."

—in his article "Global Warming is Reversible,"
The Nation, December 10, 2007

"Fox's great idea. Climate change is the great global environmental crisis, but they want to cut or destroy the EPA."

—on the Republican presidential primary debates,
Twitter, August 6, 2015

"I understand that Republicans, including many of those running for president, are dependent on the Koch brothers, oil companies and other fossil-fuel contributors. Maybe for once they can overcome the needs of their campaign contributors and worry instead about the planet they are leaving their kids and grandchildren and young people all over the world."

—August 3, 2015

"It is hard for me to understand how one can be concerned about climate change but not vigorously oppose the pipeline."

—on the Keystone XL Pipeline, *Twitter*, July 28, 2015

"The idea that we would allow for the transportation of 800,000 barrels of some of the dirtiest oils all over the world makes no sense to me."

—*Twitter*, July 28, 2015

"We have the moral responsibility to leave this planet habitable for our grandchildren."

—*Twitter*, August 9, 2015

"Giving up is not an option if we want to prevent irreparable harm to our planet."

—*Twitter*, July 23, 2015

HEALTH CARE

"I have spent my career fighting for something that I consider to be a human right. That human right is health care."

—*Twitter*, August 10, 2015

"The United States is the only major nation in the industrialized world that does not guarantee health care as a right to its people."

—on the 50th anniversary of Medicare, July 30, 2015

"Access to affordable health care should not depend on where you live. . . . What the United States should do is join every other major nation and recognize that health care is a right of citizenship. A Medicare-for-all, single-payer system would provide better care at less cost for more Americans."

—on Supreme Court decision in *King v. Burwell,* to uphold the Affordable Care Act, June 25, 2015

"[W]e spend far more per capita on health care with worse results than other countries. It is time that we bring about a fundamental transformation of the American health care system."

—on the 50th anniversary of Medicare, July 30, 2015

"It is unacceptable that Americans pay, by far, the highest prices in the world for prescription drugs. For years, generic drugs have made it possible for people to buy the medicine they need at lower prices. We need to make certain that generics remain affordable."

—on the Medicaid Generic Drug Price
Fairness Act, May 18, 2015

"Our nation's veterans cannot and should not be denied treatment while drug companies rake in billions of dollars in profits . . . We must not allow corporate greed to stand in the way of this potential."

—on the failure of Veterans Affairs to continue providing
treatment for veterans with hepatitis C, May 12, 2015

"The current attempt to discredit Planned Parenthood is part of a long-term smear campaign by people who want to deny women in this country the right to control their own bodies."

—Statement on Planned Parenthood, July 29, 2015

"The Family and Medical Leave Act we signed into law in 1993 is inadequate for the task. Today, according to the Department of Labor, nearly eight out of ten workers who are eligible to take time off under this law cannot do so because they can't afford it. Even worse, 40 percent of American workers aren't even eligible for this unpaid leave."

—"The Middle Class: It's Time to Support Real Family Values," www.berniesanders.com, June 17, 2015

"All over this country, people are becoming more conscious about the foods they are eating and the foods they are serving to their kids and this is certainly true for genetically engineered foods. I believe that when a mother goes to the store and purchases food for her child, she has the right to know what she is feeding her child. Monsanto and other major corporations should not get to decide this, the people and their elected representatives should."

—"Sanders: Let States Require GMO Food Labels,"
www.sanders.senate.gov, May 22, 2013

"You have deregulated the GMO industry from court oversight, which is really not what America is about. You should not be putting riders that people aren't familiar with, in a major piece of legislation."

—on the Monsanto Protection Act, May 28, 2013

"This is unacceptable. Until we put patients over profits, our system will not work for ordinary Americans."

—on prescription drug prices and the need to expand Medicare, July 30, 2015

"There is no job in this country that is more demanding, more important, and more fulfilling than being a nurse. You take care of our young children . . . You take care of the elderly . . . You take care of our veterans . . . And, you give people the hope that they will live to see a better day."

—Remarks at National Nurses
United Endorsement, August 10, 2015

"A large single-payer system already exists in the United States. It's called Medicare and the people enrolled give it high marks."

—*Twitter*, August 10, 2015

INTERNATIONAL
RELATIONS

"American workers deserve a trade policy that works for them and not only for the CEOs of major multi-national corporations. We cannot continue trade policies which outsource good jobs to low-wage countries overseas and lead us into a race to the bottom."

—on the Senate's decision to deny President Obama trade promotion authority, June 23, 2015

"I know of a number of members who voted for NAFTA who now see that vote as a mistake. I know of no member who voted against NAFTA who regrets that vote."

—on NAFTA, in his article "The View from Mexico," *The Nation*, January 15, 2004

"I am expressing solidarity with the people of Greece in a time of cruel and counter-productive policies ... The people of Greece are being told their voices are not being heard. Their misery does not matter. That democracy itself does not matter."

—on the Greek financial crisis,
2015 International Association of Sheet Metal,
Air, Rail, and Transportation Workers
Conference, July 28, 2015

"Let us not forget, after World War I, the Allies imposed oppressive austerity on Germany as part of the Versailles Treaty. As a result, unemployment skyrocketed, the people suffered, and the policies of austerity gave rise to the Nazi Party. We cannot let a situation like that ever happen again."

—on the Greek financial crisis in his statement to
The Huffington Post, July 28, 2015

"I believe that trade is good but we need a new approach that benefits the working families and not just corporate America."

—"Sanders Statement on House Trade Vote,"
www.sanders.senate.gov, June 18, 2015

"I am glad to hear that the State Department has removed Cuba from their list of state-sponsored terrorists. This is a major step forward in rebuilding our relationship with Cuba. I applaud President Barack Obama for moving aggressively to develop normal diplomatic relations with Cuba and I look forward to our countries building a strong friendship."

—on the State Department's removal of Cuba from the state-sponsored terrorist list, May 29, 2015

"Fifty years of Cold War is enough. It is time for Cuba and the United States to turn the page and normalize relations."

—*Twitter*, July 1, 2015

"Nike epitomizes why disastrous unfettered free trade policies during the past four decades have failed American workers."

—May 12, 2015

"Since the implementation of NAFTA, the number of Mexicans living below the poverty line has increased by over 14 million people."

—*Twitter*, August 12, 2015

"Unfettered free trade has been a disaster not only for Americans but for the working people of Mexico and Canada as well. Our difficult but important job now is to build a new coalition of trade unionists, environmentalists, small-business owners and manufacturers who put the people in their communities ahead of corporate America's reckless search for profits."

—on NAFTA, in his article "The View from Mexico," *The Nation*, January 15, 2004

"If we join together we can create trade policies that expand the middle class in this country, protect the international environment and improve the lives of poor people in developing countries. Together, we can and must end the disastrous race to the bottom that we are currently experiencing."

—on NAFTA, in his article "The View from Mexico," *The Nation*, January 15, 2004

"The political goal is to convey to the Nicaraguan people that in my view, a majority of Americans do not believe it's appropriate for the United States to unilaterally overthrow governments that it dislikes. What's happening in Nicaragua goes far beyond Nicaragua. It is symptomatic of what the United States will be in terms of its relationship with the entire world."

—to the *Burlington Free Press*, on his visit to Nicaragua, July 16, 1985

"The test of a great nation is not how many wars it can engage in, but how it can resolve international conflicts in a peaceful manner."

—on the Iran nuclear deal, *Twitter*, August 7, 2015

"The war in Iraq, which I opposed, destabilized the entire region, helped create the Islamic State, cost the lives of 6,700 brave men and women and resulted in hundreds of thousands of others in our armed forces returning home with post-traumatic-stress disorder and traumatic brain injuries. I fear that many of my Republican colleagues do not understand that war must be a last resort, not the first resort."

—on the Iran nuclear deal, *Twitter*, August 7, 2015

"The war in Iraq was one of the biggest foreign policy mistakes in modern history. I voted against military action in Iraq. It was the right choice then, and I stand by that vote today."

—May 14, 2015

"We must fundamentally rewrite our trade policy so that American products, not American jobs, are our No. 1 export."

—*Twitter*, August 3, 2015

"[T]he United States has to negotiate with other countries. We have to negotiate with Iran. And the alternative of not reaching an agreement, you know what it is? It's war. Do we really want another war, a war with Iran?"

—on the Iran nuclear deal, August 9, 2015

"The global economy is simply unsustainable when so few have so much and so many have so little."

—on the Greek debt crisis, *YouTube*, August 3, 2015

"I have spoken out consistently against the barbaric war in Vietnam and against our entire foreign policy of support to military dictatorships throughout the world. Not only is our foreign policy morally bankrupt—but it is bankrupting us financially. We spend more on the military every day than we spend on the entire budget for the state of Vermont for a year. Let us stop the war now and build low cost housing, provide free and excellent medical and dental care for all, and clean up the environment. We have the wealth and resources in this country to provide a decent standard of living for every man, woman, and child. Let's do it."

—while campaigning for US Senate,
"A Letter from Bernie Sanders," *The Freeman*, 1972

IMMIGRATION

"America has always been a haven for the oppressed. We cannot and must not shirk the historic role of the United States as a protector of vulnerable people fleeing persecution."

—*Twitter*, June 21, 2015

"We cannot continue to run an economy where millions are made so vulnerable because of their undocumented status."

—*Twitter*, August 12, 2015

"It is time to bring our neighbors out of the shadows. It is time to give them legal status. It is time to create a reasonable and responsible path to citizenship."

—*Twitter,* June 24, 2015

"We must recognize DREAMers for who they are—American kids who deserve the right to legally be in the country they know as home."

—*Twitter,* June 19, 2015

"We cannot and we should not even be talking about sweeping up millions of men, women, and children and throwing them out of the country."

—on immigration, *Twitter*, August 7, 2015

"The real symbol of America is not the barbed wire fence. It is the Statue of Liberty."

—at national conference of the
National Council of La Raza, July 13, 2015

"We have to fight against this politics of division that seeks to divide working families, that disrespects hard work, that disrespects the contributions immigrant workers make to our economy. This politics of division doesn't fix anything; it just makes it easier to exploit millions of workers who are vulnerable because of their undocumented status. We have to address that exploitation and end it. We also have to speak about who benefits from that exploitation: the same corporations that we see pushing these race-to-the-bottom policies."

—Interview, "Bernie Sanders Speaks,"
The Nation, July 6, 2015

EDUCATION

"If we could bail out Wall Street, we can make sure that every American can go to college without going into debt."

—*Twitter*, August 10, 2015

"We live in a highly competitive global economy. If our economy is to be strong, we need the best educated work force in the world. That will not happen if every year hundreds of thousands of bright young people cannot afford to go to college and if millions more leave school deeply in debt."

—on his College for All Act, May 19, 2015

"We have got to make sure that every qualified American in this country who wants to go to college can go to college—regardless of income."

—Statement on the College for All Act, May 19, 2015

"We once led the world in the percentage of our people with a college degree, now we are in 12th place. Countries like Germany, Denmark, Sweden and many more are providing free or inexpensive higher education for their young people. They understand how important it is to be investing in their youth. We should be doing the same."

—on his College for All Act, May 19, 2015

"We must revolutionize our nation's higher education system. We must invest in the young people today, because they are our nation's future doctors, teachers, engineers, scientists and senators—so they can ensure our economy and our nation as a whole have an edge in the 21st Century."

—Statement on the College for All Act, May 19, 2015

"We must convince students that if they participate in the political process we can lower the outrageously high student debt they face."

—*Twitter*, July 26, 2015

"If we were to reduce the President's proposed increase in military spending by less than half, and instead invest that money in educational opportunities for today's college students, we could cut tuition by 55 percent. So I challenge all of you . . . ask yourselves, where should our priorities lie?"

—on federal spending, speech delivered at the University of Iowa, February 2015

"Psychologists tell us that, in terms of human development, the most important years are birth through four years of age. Yet, in terms of early childhood education, our nation does a very inadequate job in making quality pre-kindergarten education available to working families."

—on the need for federal grants for early childhood education, December 23, 2013

Education

"[O]ne thing that will help kids stay in school is if they have a belief that they will be able to get a college education. For too many families college seems like an impossibility. We have got to change that. We need to give our children, regardless of their race or their income, a fair shot at attending college. That's why I support making all public universities tuition free."

—Remarks at the Southern Christian Leadership Conference, July 25, 2015

CRIMINAL JUSTICE

"The chants are growing louder. People are angry. I am angry. And people have a right to be angry. Violence and brutality of any kind, particularly at the hands of law enforcement sworn to protect and serve our communities, is unacceptable and must not be tolerated."

—on the deaths of unarmed African Americans at the hands of police, remarks at the Southern Christian Leadership Conference, July 25, 2015

"No one should have to worry that a routine interaction with law enforcement will end in violence or death."

—*Twitter*, July 25, 2015

"A growing number of communities throughout this country do not trust the police, and police have become disconnected from the communities they are sworn to protect. When I was mayor of Burlington, Vermont, the largest city in the state, one of the things we did—and I believe this very strongly—is we moved toward community policing. Community policing means that police are part of the community, not seen as oppressors in the community, and that is the direction that we have got to move.

"Sandra Bland, Michael Brown, Eric Garner, Walter Scott, Freddie Gray, we know their names. Each of them died unarmed at the hands of police officers or in police custody. Let us all be very clear, violence and brutality of any kind particularly at the hands of law enforcement sworn to protect and serve their communities is unacceptable and must not be tolerated.

"We must reform our criminal justice system. Black lives do matter, and we must value black lives."

—Remarks at National Urban League Conference, July 31, 2015

"It is not a coincidence that we have outrageously high youth unemployment rates while at the same time we have more people in jail than any other country on earth. Maybe, just maybe, we should be providing jobs and education to our young people rather than spending more and more money on jails and incarceration."

—Remarks to the Senate on child poverty and youth unemployment, July 8, 2015

"The time has come for us to begin investing in jobs and education for our kids, not jails and incarceration. Let's create productive citizens in America, not more criminals."

—Remarks to the Senate on youth unemployment, July 16, 2015

"It is no great secret that without work, without education, and without hope, people get into trouble. And the result is that tragically we have more people in jail today than any other country on Earth including China—an authoritarian Communist country with a population four times our size."

—Statement on Employ Young Americans Act,
June 4, 2015

"Today, the United States is 5 percent of the world's population, yet we have 25 percent of the world's prisoners."

—Statement on Employ Young Americans Act,
June 4, 2015

"But this [imprisonment] crisis is not just a destruction of human life, it is also very, very costly to the taxpayers of our country. In America now we spend nearly $200 billion on public safety, including $70 billion on correctional facilities each and every year . . . in my view it makes a lot more sense to invest in jobs, in job training, and in education than spending incredible amounts of money on jails and law enforcement."

—Statement on Employ Young Americans Act,
June 4, 2015

"I find it strange that the kid who smokes marijuana gets arrested but the crooks on Wall Street get off scot free."

—*Twitter*, August 3, 2015

"It is an obscenity that we stigmatize so many young Americans with a criminal record for smoking marijuana, but not one major Wall Street executive has been prosecuted for causing the near collapse of our entire economy."

—Remarks at the Southern Christian Leadership Conference, July 25, 2015

"The measure of success for law enforcement should not be how many people get locked up."

—*Twitter*, August 4, 2015

DOMESTIC CONCERNS

Senior Citizens

"The hatred of Social Security from the right-wing antigovernment crowd is based on the fact that Social Security, a government program, has been enormously successful in accomplishing its mission. For seventy-five years, in good times and bad, Social Security has provided financial security for tens of millions of Americans."

—in his article "Hands Off Social Security,"
The Nation, September 30, 2010

"Social Security can pay every penny owed for next 18 years. Lift the cap on taxable income and it'll be solvent for decades."

—on the Republican presidential primary debates,
Twitter, August 6, 2015

"One of the worst ideas is to privatize Social Security. After the greed and recklessness of Wall Street caused markets to collapse in 2008, does anyone still seriously believe it would be a good idea to turn the retirement security of millions of Americans over to Wall Street CEOs whose dishonesty and irresponsibility have no end?"

—in his article "Hands Off Social Security,"
The Nation, September 30, 2010

"We must make certain that seniors and people with disabilities can live in dignity."

—*Twitter*, July 21, 2015

"I think from a moral perspective, from a cost perspective, we want to make sure all seniors in this country, regardless of income, have the nutrition they need."

—Senate statement on accessibility of SNAP to seniors, May 22, 2013

"Social Security has been the most successful federal program in modern American history. Before Social Security, about half of senior citizens lived in poverty. Today, while still too high, fewer than 10 percent live in poverty. We must oppose all efforts to cut Social Security and fight hard to expand it."

—May 10, 2015

"A nation is judged by how it cares for its most vulnerable . . . American seniors should have the supports available to them to remain in their homes and communities. They deserve to live with dignity and with a sense of security, and the Older Americans Act helps to provide that."

—on the reauthorization of the
Older Americans Act, July 16, 2015

Media

"Much of the corporate media is prepared to discuss everything except the most important issues facing our country."

—*Twitter*, August 5, 2015

"We got a collapsing middle class. We have more wealth and income inequality today than we've had since the 1920s . . . And what big money can do is put an unbelievable amount of TV and radio ads out there to deflect attention from the real issues facing the American people."

—interview with Bill Moyers, "Bernie Sanders on Breaking Big Money's Grip on Elections," *Moyers & Company*, October 31, 2014

Net Neutrality and the Internet

"This is about the free flow of information, the free flow of ideas, on the Internet. If we let corporations put a price tag on that, so that some ideas move more quickly than other ideas because a billionaire is paying for an advantage, that changes the debate in a way that harms democracy. This is common sense . . . These fights over communication policy are really fights about how our democracy is going to function—if it is going to function—in the 21st century."

—interview, "Bernie Sanders Speaks,"
The Nation, July 6, 2015

"Given the lack of incentive for companies to provide better quality service and competitive prices, it is no surprise that individuals rank cable and Internet providers last in customer satisfaction when compared to other companies in other industries . . . We need healthy competition to foster innovation and ensure fair prices for consumers. At the very least, Americans should be able to understand the price of the product they are buying and what their neighbors are paying for the same service."

—on cable and Internet companies,
Federal Communications Commission Letter
to Chairman Tom Wheeler, July 9, 2015

Military Services

"If you are not prepared to take care of the men and women who put their lives on the line to defend this country—who came back wounded in body, wounded in spirit—if you're not prepared to help those people, then don't send them to war in the first place."

—May 25, 2015

"To my mind, it is simply unacceptable if the brave men and women in our military, who are willing to risk their lives to defend this country, do not feel comfortable reporting a sexual assault or do not believe the military would adequately respond to such a report. While the military chain of command works extraordinary well for dealing with most infractions, I personally believe the reporting and prosecution of certain crimes should be taken out of the chain of command structure."

—Statement at the Joint Hearing Committee
on General, Housing and Military Affairs,
and Senate Committee on Government Operations,
Military Sexual Assault, January 30, 2014

Infrastructure

"It is no secret that our infrastructure is crumbling . . . One of every nine bridges in our country is structurally deficient and nearly a quarter are functionally obsolete. Almost one-third of our roads are in poor or mediocre condition."

—on the need to increase infrastructure funding,
June 24, 2015

"Moreover, at a time when real unemployment is near 11 percent, we need jobs and we need them now . . . We can fix our roads and bridges and put Americans back to work at the same time."

—on the need to increase infrastructure funding,
June 24, 2015

Gun Rights

"Nobody should have a gun who has a criminal background or who's involved in domestic abuse situations."

—*Twitter*, July 31, 2015

"Certain types of guns exclusively used to kill people, not for hunting, should not be sold in America."

—*Twitter*, August 1, 2015

"I come from a state that has virtually no gun control and it turns out to be one of the safest states in the country. I come from a state where tens and tens of thousands of people hunt and do target practice. I understand that guns in my state are different than guns in Chicago or Los Angeles. People in urban America have got to appreciate that the overwhelming majority of people who hunt know about guns and respect guns, and are law-abiding people, that's the truth. And people in rural America have got to understand that in an urban area, guns mean something very, very different."

—on gun control, July 10, 2015

"There is no single or simple solution to this crisis. In my view, Congress must consider a comprehensive approach which includes a serious discussion about guns, the need for greatly expanded mental health services and ending gratuitous violence [in] the media."

—on gun control, May 13, 2015

164

Privacy

"We must keep our country safe and protect ourselves from terrorists, but we can do that without undermining the constitutional and privacy rights which make us a free nation."

—on legislation to extend domestic spying programs, June 2, 2015

"I believe we need to take a look at how the public and private sectors are gathering data on the American people and how we are moving toward an Orwellian society in which your location and movements can be tracked at any time through your smartphones and computers."

—on legislation to extend domestic
spying programs, June 2, 2015